LET THE CHILDREN COME TO ME

Nurturing Anabaptist Faith Within Families

Lisa Weaver & Elizabeth Miller

Design by Judith Rempel Smucker

Cascadia

Publishing House
Telford, Pennsylvania

Cascadia Publishing House orders, information, reprint permissions:
contact@CascadiaPublishingHouse.com
1-215-723-9125
126 Klingerman Road, Telford PA 18969
https://www.CascadiaPublishingHouse.com

Let the Children Come to Me
Copyright © 2018 by Cascadia Publishing House,
a division of Cascadia Publishing House LLC
Telford PA 18969
All rights reserved.
Library of Congress Catalog Number: 2018045343
ISBN-13: 9781680270136; **ISBN 10:** 1680270133
Design by Judith Rempel Smucker

Library of Congress Cataloging-in-Publication Data
Names: Weaver, Lisa D., author. | Miller, Elizabeth, 1984- author.
Title: Let the children come to me : nurturing Anabaptist faith within
   families / Lisa Weaver and Elizabeth Miller.
Description: Telford, Pennsylvania : Cascadia Publishing House, [2018]
Identifiers: LCCN 2018045343| ISBN 9781680270136 (8 x 8" trade pbk. : alk.
   paper) | ISBN 1680270133 (8 x 8" trade pbk. : alk. paper)
Subjects: LCSH: Anabaptists—Doctrines. | Christian education—
Home training. | Children—Religious life. | Faith development.
   Classification: LCC BX4931.3 .W428 2018 | DDC 248.4/843—dc23
LC record available at https://lccn.loc.gov/2018045343

25 24 23 22 21 20 19   8 7 6 5 4 3 2 1

Jesus said, "Let the little children come to me, and do not stop them; for it is to such as these that the kingdom of heaven belongs."
Matthew 19:14

as a hen gathers her brood under wings...

How often have I desired to gather your children together as a hen gathers her brood under her wings.
Matthew 23:37b

CONTENTS

Introduction 4

1 Scripture reading
6

2 Prayer
10

3 Community
14

4 Bearing witness
18

5 Worship
22

6 Nonviolence
26

7 Steadfast faith
30

8 Centrality of Jesus
34

9 Communion
38

10 Believers baptism
42

11 Service to one another
46

12 Stewardship
50

Afterword 55 / Suggestions for use in Christian Education 56
Acknowledgments 59 / Credits and permissions 60

INTRODUCTION

WELCOME to a time of family faith development. We hope that the stories, scriptures, prayers, and activities suggested in this resource will deepen Anabaptist values of peace, community, and service, and nurture a love of Jesus growing within the hearts and minds of young people. In Matthew 19:14 Jesus says: "Let the little children come to me, and do not stop them; for it is to such as these that the kingdom of heaven belongs." Blessings to your family as you walk this faith journey together.

Here are some specific considerations as you prepare for this family time:

WHO IS PRESENT?

Perhaps you want to keep this time special for the people who live together in your house. Maybe you want to invite an extended family member (grandparent, cousin, aunt, or uncle) who lives in the area. Another possibility would be to embark upon this faith journey with another family from your congregation, sharing a community experience together each week or month. Or is there a neighbor or friend who has expressed interest in your faith?

HOW OFTEN?

There are twelve units in this resource, so it would be possible to set aside one evening a month, stretching out the experience over a calendar year. Other families may choose to have a certain day of each week to focus on the stories. Another option would be to use this resource when your family has extra time, such as a vacation break from the school year, a relaxed week away from home, or when grandparents come to visit. There are lovely benefits of multi-generational conversations.

Here are a few tips for accessing the different sections of the units:

INTRO/DEFINITIONS:

As you gather each week, you may decide to start by naming the practice that is the focal point for each unit. Before reading the definition, it is interesting to learn what children already understand of the idea and what connections come to their minds. This is a wonderful opportunity to share examples from your home, family, or church life where this practice is already in place.

Stories can bring peace and healing to our world.

—César García, Secretary General of Mennonite World Conference (August 5-8, 2012, Bearing Witness Consultation at Goshen College)

STORYTELLING:

There are many ways to share the stories found in this resource. Here are a few options to consider:

▶ Explain that there will be two stories for each theme—one from the sixteenth century, and one from contemporary times.
▶ Use a map or globe to identify where the stories take place.
▶ The text can be read aloud by an adult or a child.
▶ You may choose to take turns pointing out what is in the accompanying photos or illustrations.
▶ Perhaps children would like to draw while the stories are being read. Share their pictures when they are done.

SCRIPTURE:

This is an excellent opportunity to help children learn how to find scripture texts in the Bible. Look at the list of books in the Old and New Testaments. What names do they recognize from Sunday School? If desired, allow children to underline the scripture verse they find each time or use sticky notes to mark the books as they are found. It is interesting to compare different translations of the same verse.

FAMILY QUESTIONS:

It might work to pass a small object around the circle when answering questions in a group. The idea is that everyone in the circle is actively listening to whomever is holding the "talking piece." This gives even the quieter or more hesitant speakers a turn to share. It also may be helpful to suggest a moment of quiet thinking before answers are given. A young child or a new speaker may like to whisper-talk with an adult before sharing out loud.

PRAYER:

There are many ways to share a prayer at the closing of your time. Options would include:

▶ Join hands, and have an adult read the prayer.
▶ Have an adult say a phrase, and have children echo line by line.
▶ Use the printed prayer as an opening sentence and allow everyone to add his or her own sentence of thanks.

Further note:

If your family enjoys music, you may choose to open or close your family time with a favorite song or hymn.

1. SCRIPTURE READING

Scriptures are holy writings. For Christians, the Bible is Scripture. The Old Testament tells the story of the people of Israel. The New Testament continues the story by describing the life of Jesus and the beginnings of the Christian church.

EARLY STORY

Elizabeth Dirks lived in the Netherlands in the 1500s. As a young girl, she was sent to a convent to live and study to become a nun. When she was twelve years old, Elizabeth heard the story of a man who belonged to a group of people called Anabaptists. This man had read the Bible for himself. For the first time in more than a thousand years, Bibles were available in the languages that common people spoke. This man began to question the rules of the established church and was thus arrested and killed for his beliefs.

This story made a deep impression on Elizabeth and inspired her to find and read the New Testament for herself. Eventually, Elizabeth decided she wanted to leave the convent and join the Anabaptists, but she had to do so secretly without telling anyone where she was going. She disguised herself by wearing a set of clothes borrowed from a milkmaid and snuck out of the convent.

Elizabeth joined an Anabaptist community and later became a leader in the church. She wrote these words, which can be found in the *Martyrs Mirror:* "All the waters in the sea could not save me, but salvation is in Christ (Acts 4:10), and He has commanded me to love God my Lord above all things, and my neighbor as myself."

(from *Martyrs Mirror,* page 482)

A 500-year-old Bible and a modern day Bible.

6

Samuel Kakesa was a Mennonite church leader from Bandundu Province in the Republic of Congo. In 1964 Pierre Mulele and his soldiers started a war against the government, threatening many of the people who lived in the Bandundu Province. One day, this group of rebel soldiers captured Samuel and took him to their camp. In the camp Samuel was forced to work typing messages for the group's leader, Pierre Mulele.

"What am I doing?" Samuel asked himself. "I'm contributing to the destruction of my own homeland and the enslavement of my own people. I'm being used by this evil movement." Escape from the rebel camp was impossible, but Samuel determined to find some way to show that he had not renounced his faith or his God.

One day a visitor was able to smuggle a New Testament to him, hidden in a packet of clothing. Every evening Samuel walked away from the camp, sat on a fallen log, and read his New Testament. Even after his habit was discovered by Pierre Mulele, Samuel trusted God and went to the same spot every night to read the Scriptures.

Samuel was eventually released from the camp and continued to serve in the Congo Mennonite Church for many years.

Samuel Kakesa with his family.

? FAMILY QUESTIONS

▶ Where do you hear Bible stories?

▶ With whom do you read Bible stories?

▶ Which story is your favorite?

▶ Why do you think reading the Bible was so important to Elizabeth Dirks and Samuel Kakesa?

ACTIVITY

SCRIPTURE

Luke 4:16-17a

When Jesus came to Nazareth, where he had been brought up, he went to the synagogue on the sabbath day, as was his custom. He stood up to read, and the scroll of the prophet Isaiah was given to him.

READ OR MEMORIZE a scripture passage together.

Place a small item (a bead, shell, or stone) in a basket or bowl as you learn or say each verse. Each member of the circle can read or memorize at least one segment of the scripture, so that collectively the entire passage is spoken. Or, an adult can read the entire passage and children can take turns adding an item for each verse.

Suggestions: Matthew 5:14-16 or Psalm 23

FIND IT!

Choose a scripture passage that connects to a particular time of the year (Luke 2:8-20) or a passage that was or will be read in your congregation's weekly worship service.

PRAYER

Thank you, God, for stories and messages in the Bible, and for the people who read those words to me.

Amen

EXTEND IT!

Instead of a scripture passage, try this activity with the words of a favorite hymn or camp song.

2. PRAYER

Prayer is communication with God. A prayer can be words spoken to God or a time of listening to God. A prayer of thanks is often said before a meal. People can pray together silently or join their voices together in song. Prayers can be actions, such as the lighting of a candle, caring for a person in need, or tending a garden.

EARLY STORY

The Philippites were a group of Anabaptists living in Moravia in the sixteenth century. They were treated harshly because of their Anabaptist faith, so a group of about fifty Philippites finally decided they would leave and look for a safer place to live. As they were fleeing, their group was captured and imprisoned in a dungeon in the fortress of Passau. While in prison, members of this group wrote a number of hymns. The hymns they wrote are similar to the Psalms we read in the Bible. Some of these hymns are found in the Ausbund, the hymnal used by the Amish today.

Hymn #314 in the 1992 North American Mennonite *Hymnal: A Worship Book* is a translation of one of the hymns written by the Anabaptists imprisoned in Passau. In this hymn, the Philippites praise God for how God has given them strength and joy, even in prison. These hymns can be sung today as prayers to God, asking for comfort and steadfast faith in difficult times.

The word of God is solid ground,
our constant firm confession.
No source of freedom more profound,
no purer a profession.
All steadfast strength,
all breadth and length of truth,
from God's word springing
Shall we employ to speak our joy,
this world our witness bringing.

GLOBAL STORY

Hilda Franz was living in Manitoba, Canada, when her beloved husband died. Her niece knit her a prayer shawl, of beautiful beige and brown yarn, to comfort her.

Hilda missed her husband very much, and she wore the shawl constantly. She wore it in her house and put it on over her jacket if she went outdoors. Its warmth reminded her of Psalm 125:2: "As the mountains surround Jerusalem, so the Lord surrounds His people from this time on and forever." Hilda felt loved and supported by all of the prayers around her.

A year after she had been given the shawl, Hilda made a long trip across the country to visit friends. When her friends picked her up at the bus station, Hilda accidentally left her shawl on the ledge where she had been sitting.

When Hilda realized she had left the shawl behind, she went back to get it. But it was not there. Hilda looked and looked, but she finally had to admit to herself that she would not get the shawl back. Instead she prayed to God that whomever had the shawl now would be blessed by God.

Hilda Franz, age seventy-four, first learned about prayer shawls at a Native Assembly gathering in 2006. At this gathering, she was given two shawls to take back to her home congregation to give away. Since then she has knit numerous shawls herself. While she knits, she prays for the person who will be receiving the shawl.

Sometimes very special things are removed from us, but life goes on. I still think periodically about that shawl and pray for the person who has it. The person may not know that it is a prayer shawl, but God knows it is a prayer shawl.
—Hilda Franz

FAMILY QUESTIONS

▶ When do you pray?
▶ Where do you pray?
▶ How do you feel when you pray?
▶ What happens to your body and your heart when you pray?

Matthew 6:9b-12

**Our Father in heaven,
Hallowed be
your name.
Your kingdom come.
Your will be done,
on earth as it is
in heaven.
Give us this day
our daily bread.
And forgive us our
debts as we also
have forgiven our
debtors.**

ACTIVITY

SHARE A BLESSING with each other. Purchase, make, or use a favorite blanket, shawl, or cloth. Place it around the shoulders of the person beside you, saying, "May you feel the love of God wrap around you like this blanket." Continue until everyone has had a turn to say and receive the blessing.

MAKE IT!

Directions for a simple fleece blanket:

1. Cut two pieces of fleece, each to the same desired size. (The finished blanket will be the size of one of the pieces.)

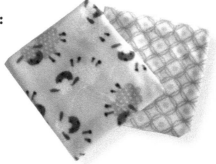

2. Place the pieces back-to-back, patterned sides out.

3. With a fabric scissors, make three-inch cuts, one inch apart, around the edges. Cut through both pieces of fabric at once, so that the resulting fringe lines up exactly. The corners should be cut and removed as shown in the photo.

 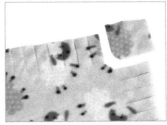

4. Tie a knot, using one flap from each fleece, all around the edges. A double knot will hold securely.

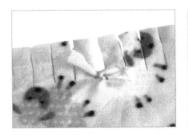 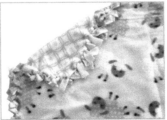

5. Your blanket is finished!

PRAYER

Thank you, God, for hearing our prayers.

Amen

3. COMMUNITY

The church is a community of people linked together to one another and to God. That linking is shown in community worship and gatherings. Community members support each other in daily life, in times of both joy and sorrow.

EARLY STORY

A group of Anabaptists lived in the town of Nikolsburg in Moravia. They called themselves the *Stäbler*, because instead of carrying a sword, this pacifist group chose to carry a staff—*Stab* in German.

In the winter of 1528, the *Stäbler* were expelled from Nikolsburg. They decided they would walk to the city of Austerlitz, where it was safe to be an Anabaptist. Because the trek would be long and difficult, they knew that they would have to cooperate in order to survive. So the *Stäbler* gathered all of their belongings on a blanket on the frozen ground. They decided that they would share everything together, so that each person would have what was needed.

Once they reached Moravia, this practice of sharing food, clothing, and other belongings continued and became known as the *community of goods.*

A modern-day staff

14

Parrapat, India

GLOBAL STORY

In 2008, 3,000 people gathered to celebrate fifty years of Bible festivals in Parrapat, India.

Participants gathered at the Mennonite church in Basna for a prayer service, before leaving on a two-mile walk to Parrapat. Singing, dancing, and fireworks accompanied the walkers.

Barkat Chandu, whose grandmother was one of the first Mennonites in India, said the public march was a form of witness. Mahendre Kulbeep, a leader in the Bhartiya General Conference Mennonite Church, said, "This is a peace rally. By this rally, we are leaving a message for the name and hand of Jesus."

The *mela* lasted for five days and included many competitions—for best traditional and contemporary songs, praise dances, and debates. Youth competed in Bible memorization, learning the book of 1 Peter by heart.

FAMILY QUESTIONS

▶ What does your community or congregation share with each other?

▶ What do you share with your neighbors?

▶ Can you remember a time when someone shared something with you or made you feel included?

MAKE OR WRITE A CARD to send to someone in your congregation or community. Maybe your card will go to: a neighbor, your pastor or Sunday School teacher, or someone who has been sick or in the hospital.

Accordion card:

1. Cut an 8 ½ x 11 inch sheet of paper in half lengthwise, to create a strip that is 4 ¼ x 11 inches.
2. Fold the paper in half, then half again.
3. Unfold, so that the paper has four small segments on each side.

1 Corinthians 12:26

If one member suffers, all suffer together with it; if one member is honored, all rejoice together with it.

Each member of the circle can write a favorite scripture verse or message, or illustrate one segment of the card. Or each person can make an accordion to give away!

Pop-out card:

1. Cut an 8 ½ x 11 inch sheet of paper in half, to create a piece that is 8 ½ x 5 ½ inches.

2. Fold the paper in half.
3. Make two parallel cuts, each one inch long, in the middle of the folded edge.

4. When you open the card, press the little flap in, so that it pops out to the middle of the card.
5. Using another scrap of paper, make a shape to glue or tape onto the pop-out flap, so that it stands out when the card is opened.

6. This shape can be decorated with illustrations, a scripture verse, or a personal message.
7. Glue the decorated piece onto a slightly larger piece of paper of contrasting color.

PRAYER

Thank you, God, for neighbors, friends, and our church family.

Amen

17

4. BEARING WITNESS

Anabaptists have a history of "bearing witness" to their faith in Jesus, even in difficult circumstances. Bearing witness may mean that a person continues to live out her or his faith even when it is against the law. For some, bearing witness means participating in a public action to show a way of thinking, believing, or being. Others would explain bearing witness as a way of living each day, no matter how ordinary, as a disciple of Christ.

EARLY STORY

Joriaen Simon, an Anabaptist living in the Netherlands, was a weaver and a bookseller who owned and distributed Anabaptist books. In a letter that Joriaen wrote to his son, he described the beginning of his life as "unprofitable, proud, puffed-up, drunken, selfish, deceitful, and full of all manner of idolatry." Joriaen goes on to say, however, that when he began to read the Scriptures, his life changed. He took the Word of God as his counselor, abandoned his former life, and became a follower of Christ within the Anabaptist community.

In 1557 Joriaen was arrested and killed. City officials brought out Joriaen's books to be burned, because they did not want anyone else to read them. But when the books were thrown into the fire, the crowd rushed forward and grabbed the books out of the flames. The books were flung out among the people, where they were eagerly grasped and taken home.

Though the city officials had tried to do the opposite, the Anabaptist books were shared among the people, where they were read, discussed, and taken to heart.

(from *Martyrs Mirror,* pages 563-568)

In 1985, **Hugo Donatti** worked for a state-owned electrical company in the city of La Paz, Uruguay. All state workers like Hugo had to pledge their loyalty to the national flag and participate in an annual flag ceremony.

After joining the Mennonite church, Hugo began to question the practice of pledging loyalty or swearing allegiance to a flag. In his own Bible study and in conversation with other congregation members, he began to think about the Sermon on the Mount that says, "Do not swear at all" (Matt. 5:34). Hugo started to wonder if he should refuse to participate in the upcoming flag ceremony.

When the day of the flag ceremony neared, it was announced that anyone who did not participate would lose one month's paycheck. Hugo's family needed the money he earned, but Hugo was sincere in his desire to follow the teachings in the Bible. He talked about his dilemma with others in his church. The church members told Hugo they would support him. They even said they would help pay his bills in the month he would not receive his paycheck. Hugo decided he would not participate in the flag ceremony.

When Hugo announced his decision, his boss surprised him by asking questions about Hugo's faith. Then his boss shared about some of his own personal struggles. When their conversation ended, Hugo's boss said, "You are the kind of employee we need here. You won't need to participate in the Flag Day ceremony. And don't worry. I'll see to it that your monthly paycheck is not withheld."

Hugo's faithfulness to God's kingdom opened up surprising new ways for Hugo to share his story with those around him.

Hugo and his wife Mabel became co-pastors of La Lucha Mennonite Church. Mabel became active in the Latin American Movement of Women Theologians and in Mennonite World Conference. The story told here took place when Hugo was a new Mennonite, around thirty years old.

FAMILY QUESTIONS

▶ How does your church share the message of Jesus?

▶ How does your family bear witness to (or share) God's love?

SCRIPTURE

Matthew 5:14-16

You are the light of the world. A city built on a hill cannot be hid. No one after lighting a lamp puts it under the bushel basket, but on the lampstand, and it gives light to all in the house. In the same way, let your light shine before others, so that they may see your good works and give glory to your Father in heaven.

BEAR WITNESS to the ways that family members bring the light and love of Christ to each other.

TALK ABOUT IT!

Gather in a circle.

Choose an object to pass around the circle. You may choose to have an object connected with light (eg. a flashlight, a candle, a Star of Bethlehem ornament) or it may just be a favorite family item.

As each person takes a turn to hold the object, the others in the circle name ways in which that person brings light and love to the family. Sentence starters might include:

I sense God's love when you...
It makes me smile/laugh when you…
Thank you for…

Consider the scripture passage from Matthew 5:
"You are the light of the world."

• What are all the ways in which light is found or created?
• How do people fill their homes with light?
• How do people fill their homes with love?
• How can light be passed from one person to another?
• How can love be passed from one person to another?

PRAYER

Thank you, God, for giving us opportunities to share love with others.

Amen

21

5. WORSHIP

Worship is a time when church members come together to pray, sing, read scripture, share with each other, and give praise to God. It can be a time of fellowship, comfort, celebration, or a call for renewed action. It is a time to come together in God's presence and remember why we make Jesus the center of our lives. Believers can worship in a church building, in a home, or in a boat—worship can happen anywhere!

EARLY STORY

Pieter Pieters Beckjen (from *Martyrs Mirror*, page 739)

In the sixteenth century, it was against the law to gather as Anabaptists to worship God. Instead Anabaptists often had to meet in secret to read the Bible and sing hymns. They met in the woods, in caves, or in barns.

In the Netherlands where there were many dykes and channels of water running through the towns, Anabaptists used those spaces to worship in secret. Pieter Pieters Beckjen sometimes did his preaching in a boat, so that the authorities on shore could not see or hear what was being said.

In 1546, when Andrew Smuel and Dirk Pieters of the Netherlands were arrested for being Anabaptists, they testified that they had studied the Bible together in a place other than at church:

Question: Where did the apostles go to teach?
Answer: They went into the synagogues, and preached the Gospel of Christ.

Question: We have heard that you also teach wherever you go.
Answer: We may have read the Gospel together.

Question: Where did you read it together?
Answer: At the dyke.

(from *Martyrs Mirror*, page 477)

Left to right: Ciril Ebala, William Kulepeta, Exoce Fumana

In the Kinshasa Mennonite Church in the Congo, joyous singing and drumming are important parts of worship. To song leader and drummer William Kulepeta the different sounds the drums (*tam-tam*) make have meaning in worship.

Multiple drums are often played at the same time. Using both a tall drum (called *Ngoma* in William's region) and a smaller drum (*Kapeteng*) gives a rhythm to the music. Often the *Kapeteng* begins and the *Ngoma* drum enters later. The *Kapeteng* gives a small sound which can be compared to the notes of the higher octave. The *Ngoma* gives a heavier sound which can be compared to the notes of the lower octave.

Drums are made from a single piece of wood that is hollowed out by hand till the sides are the correct width. An animal skin—goat, cow, or antelope—is stretched across the open end of the drum.

Rev. Mumba Kabula

FAMILY QUESTIONS

▶ Where does your congregation gather for worship?

▶ What is the most unusual place you have gathered for a church service?

▶ What is your favorite part of worship?

23

ACTIVITY

SCRIPTURE

Matthew 18:20

For where two or three are gathered in my name, I am there among them.

WORSHIP TOGETHER
in an unusual place.

Depending on your location and the time of year, consider: under a tree, while on a hike, next to a favorite window, or creating a "tent" inside with chairs and a blanket.

Perhaps you will read a Bible story together, sing, pray, or share joys and concerns.

FIND IT!

MAKE IT!

Start a journal of your interesting worship places. Write down where you were, what Bible stories you read, or what you sang together. Draw a picture or have a grown-up take a photo to include in your journal.

EXTEND IT!

6. NONVIOLENCE

Anabaptists reject the use of violence, because Jesus rejected violence and told his disciples to love their enemies. Because the sword was a soldier's weapon in the sixteenth century, the early Anabaptists sometimes referred to nonviolence as the "rejection of the sword." Anabaptists seek change through prayer, faithful witness, and peaceful actions. Christian lives reflect the ultimate peace that comes from God.

EARLY STORY

Mennonites are named after **Menno Simons**, a sixteenth-century Dutch Anabaptist and pastor. In 1552 Menno wrote,

"The Prince of Peace is Christ Jesus. His kingdom is the kingdom of peace, which is His church. His messengers are the messengers of peace. His Word is the Word of peace. His body is the body of peace. His children are the seed of peace and His inheritance and reward the inheritance and reward of peace. In short, with this King, and in His kingdom and reign, it is nothing but peace. Everything that is seen, heard and done is peace."

When a group of violent Anabaptists took over the city of Munster, Menno spoke against their actions, saying:

"Christ is our fortress; patience our weapon of defense; the Word of God is our sword; and our victory a courageous, firm, unfeigned faith in Jesus Christ."

Engraving by Christoffel van Sichem

26

GLOBAL STORY

Melvin Ira Glick was a young Mennonite in the United States during the years of World War II. He was drafted to serve in the military but because of his Anabaptist belief in nonviolence decided that he could not do so.

Instead Melvin worked in an alternative service program called Civilian Public Service. He was assigned to work in a mental health hospital in Baltimore, Maryland. At this point in time, mental health patients were often treated harshly.

One day hospital administrators told Melvin that he needed to move a group of patients from one building to another. Melvin was given clubs and cattle prods and told to hand them out to the other staff members. They were to use the clubs and cattle prods to control the patients while they were moving.

In direct defiance of his orders, Melvin put away the clubs and cattle prods. Rather, he gathered several other workers and suggested that they join hands and form a circle around the group of patients. The workers had been warned that some of the patients were dangerous. But with a circle of arms and kind words to guide them, the group of patients walked calmly to their destination.

FAMILY QUESTIONS

▶ How do you show kindness to others?

▶ How do you solve problems?

▶ What other stories of peacemakers do you know?

27

SCRIPTURE

Isaiah 2:4b

They shall beat their swords into plowshares, and their spears into pruning hooks; nation shall not lift up sword against nation, neither shall they learn war any more.

Love your neighbor

CREATE A PEACE BANNER

A banner can be any size. It can be made out of a sheet of paper, poster board, felt, or the inside of a brown grocery bag.

A banner can be any shape. Consider a rectangle, circle, or triangle.

MAKE IT!

There are many ways to decorate your banner: crayons, markers, colored pencils, yarn, felt, buttons, or other craft supplies you have in your home.

What illustration or design will be on your banner? What images make you feel peaceful and happy?

Colombian Mennonites participate in a march for peace and economic justice (Pan y Paz) in Bogotá.

The golden rule

Love others as you Love yourself.

What message will your banner have? Think about a phrase from a song, a favorite scripture, or words that remind you about Jesus.

Where will you hang your banner? Choose a place that you will see often, such as a doorway, a window, or the refrigerator.

This is the day that the Lord has made. Let us rejoice and be glad in it!
Psalm 118:24

Blessed are the peacemakers, for they will be called children of God.
Matthew 5:9

Beloved, let us love one another, because love is from God and everyone who loves is born of God and knows God.
1 John 4:7-8

Thank you, God, for people who work for peace.

Amen

7. STEADFAST FAITH

A steadfast faith endures through both joyful and difficult times. Anabaptists practice their faith within a community, celebrating joys together and offering courage and strength to each other in times of difficulty. Anabaptists in the sixteenth century often faced severe persecution—including arrest, imprisonment, torture, and death; many Anabaptist communities around the world today face similar hardships.

EARLY STORY

Hadewijk was an Anabaptist woman living in the Netherlands in the 1500s. Because of her faith, she was arrested, imprisoned, and told that she would face questioning. Hadewijk was worried and afraid. While she was praying alone in her cell, Hadewijk heard a voice say her name. Looking around and seeing no one, she returned to her praying. A second time she heard her name spoken, yet she saw no one. Finally, a third time she heard the voice. This time the voice commanded, "Hadewijk, I tell thee, come out!" Hadewijk was surprised to see that the door to her cell had been opened.

Hadewijk ran out of her cell and into the streets. But where could she hide?

First Hadewijk hid in a church, but there she heard people talking about her escape from prison. Next she went to the house of some people she knew, but they were too afraid to offer her shelter. Hadewijk began to despair. As she walked passed the priest's house, however, she recognized the man standing in the doorway. This man was known to everyone in the town as being trusting and childlike. When Hadewijk asked him for help, he agreed to hide her in the attic of the priest's house and even managed to bring her food and drink.

The next morning, the man took a message to Hadewijk's brother-in-law in the market. Her brother-in-law brought a boat to the back of the priest's house where Hadewijk was waiting. Hadewijk climbed in, and the pair left through the floodgates of the city. Haedwijk fled to the city of Emden, where she lived there as part of the Anabaptist community until she was an old woman. (from *Martyrs Mirror,* pages 546-547)

In Ethiopia in the 1980s it was forbidden to be in possession of a Bible. If a person was caught with a Bible, the Bible was burned and the person could be put into prison. Mennonites in Ethiopia hid their Bibles or ripped out single pages to fold up and put in their pockets. They also memorized passages that they could then recite when they were together with other Christians.

Since it was against the law for Christians to meet together in a church building, Mennonites started meeting together in homes in very small groups. Only five people were allowed in each group, and the meeting place changed often. Some people in the church prepared Bible study materials, and they were secretly passed to all of the groups.

When the church was first forced to go into hiding, there were about 5,000 Mennonites in Ethiopia. Ten years later, the government changed and laws against religious communities were lifted. When the Mennonite church counted its community members at that point, the number had grown to 50,000. The church had been growing, one small group at a time!

Meserete Kristos Church, Addis Ababa, Ethiopia.

FAMILY QUESTIONS

▶ Have you ever been sad or afraid?

▶ Who helps you when you are worried about something?

▶ How do you offer comfort to other people?

▶ How does your church support people who are struggling with a difficult situation?

SCRIPTURE

Matthew 28:20b

**And remember,
I am with you
always, to the end
of the age.**

MAKE IT!

CREATE A SET OF "POCKET VERSES"

What verse would you like to carry with you throughout the day? Each member of the family can choose one verse to write on a slip of paper. Decorate your slip if you would like. Fold up the slip and tuck it into a pocket, purse, or even your sock or shoe! Check your verse throughout the day, whenever you like.

Jesus said to him, I am the way and the truth and the life. No one comes to the Father except through me.
— John 14:6

EXTEND IT!

At the end of the day (or the following day) gather and re-share your verses again. Perhaps you would like to trade slips so that you have a new verse to carry the next day.

8. CENTRALITY OF JESUS

A disciple is someone who learns from a teacher. Anabaptists learn from Jesus and commit to live in ways shaped by the life of Jesus. They look to scripture to see how Jesus acted and related to others. Anabaptists seek to keep Jesus as the center of their lives.

EARLY STORY

Anna Jansz was a young Dutch woman from a wealthy family who joined the Anabaptist movement in 1534. She was arrested for Anabaptist activity and, while in jail in 1539, she wrote a letter to her young son. This letter has been beloved by Anabaptists for many years. Anna speaks of the importance of following Jesus, even in difficult circumstances:

I go, I say, the way which Christ Jesus, the eternal word of the Father, full of grace and truth, the Shepherd of the sheep, who is the Life, Himself went, and who went this way and not another, and who had to drink of this cup, even as He said: 'I have a cup to drink of, and a baptism to be baptized with; and how I am straitened till it be accomplished!' Having passed through, He calls His sheep, and His sheep hear His voice, and follow Him whithersoever He goes; for this is the way of the true fountain.

(from an old letter in the *Martyrs Mirror*, pages 453-454)

Naomi Tamura is a young Mennonite Christian from Japan. In Japan there are very few Christians, so Naomi and others in her church often feel different from those around them. Some people think that those who seek to follow Christ are weak or poor.

But Naomi thinks that the differences of her faith are good. "I gave up being in the norm to live together with God," says Naomi.

Naomi likes the words of Jesus in the Sermon on the Mount (Matt. 5:9): "Blessed are the peacemakers, for they shall be called children of God." Because of Jesus' teachings and the ways he lived out peacemaking, Naomi knows that her difference as a Mennonite Christian is a good thing. When she acts as a peacemaker in the way of Jesus, people notice.

"I think that the 'difference' Japanese people feel against the peacemakers is the sign that our work is bringing change into this world," says Naomi. "They don't know God, but God knows them well. We as Christians can love them as neighbors. They can understand Jesus through working with us Christians." Naomi hopes that her life can introduce others in Japan to Jesus.

FAMILY QUESTIONS

▶ What is your favorite story of Jesus?

▶ Can you think of stories of Jesus as a baby, a young person, and a grownup?

▶ What stories of Jesus are you talking about in Sunday School or church?

▶ Why do you think Christians tell the stories of Jesus?

SCRIPTURE

I Corinthians 3:11

For no one can lay any foundation other than the one that has been laid; that foundation is Jesus Christ.

SHARE THE STORIES OF JESUS with each other.

What symbols would help you remember the stories of Jesus that you named during your "Family Questions" conversation? For example, a fish might help you remember the loaves-and-fishes story from Matthew 14:13-21; a boat might help you remember when Jesus calmed the storm in Matthew 8:23-27.

Create or gather symbols for as many stories as you would like. Consider gathering a symbol for each family member's favorite story.

FIND IT AT HOME!

SYMBOL: a manger scene
STORY: Jesus is born (Luke 2:1-7)

SYMBOL: a towel
STORY: Jesus washing his disciples' feet (John 13:3-5)

FIND IT IN NATURE!

SYMBOL: a heart
STORY: Jesus says, "Love your neighbor" and tells a story about The Good Samaritan (Luke 10:25-37)

SYMBOL: a boat
STORY: Jesus calms the storm
(Matthew 8:23-27)

Thank you, God,
for giving us Jesus,
who showed us
how to live a life
of peace.

Amen

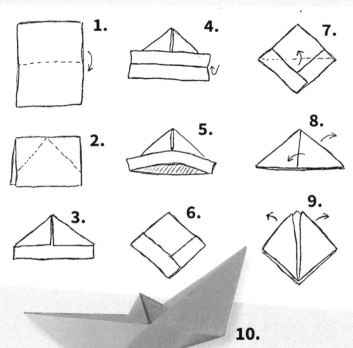

1.

2.

3.

4.

5.

6.

7.

8.

9.

10.

▶ Once you've gathered all your symbols, can you go back and name each story?

▶ What if you look at the symbols tomorrow? Would you still be able to name and tell the stories?

▶ Where can you place these symbols in your home to look at during the week?

9. COMMUNION

The Lord's Supper is the last meal that Jesus shared with his disciples before he was crucified on the cross. While eating this meal of bread and wine, Jesus said, "Do this in remembrance of me." Communion is the religious practice of sharing bread and wine (or juice) as part of a worship service.

Anabaptists in the sixteenth century differed from the state churches in their understanding of communion. Anabaptists understood the bread and cup as symbols of the body and blood of Jesus, rather than believing that an actual transformation of the elements took place. Anabaptists shared communion as a way to remember and renew their commitment to the church community and to the teachings of Jesus.

Anabaptists also began the practice of serving communion to one another, instead of requiring a priest to do so. This understanding of ministering to one another is known as the Priesthood of All Believers.

EARLY STORY

The *Martyrs Mirror* contains many court records of questions and answers about communion. In them we can see the difference between the Anabaptist understanding of communion and the way the state church viewed communion. Elizabeth Dirks was asked: "What are your views with regard to the most adorable, holy sacrament?"

Elizabeth replies: "I have never in my life read in the holy Scriptures of a holy sacrament, but of the Lord's Supper." Elizabeth was saying that eating the bread of communion was not what saved a person's soul, but that eating the bread was a reminder of the life of Jesus.

Perhaps one of the boldest answers was given in 1549, by a man named Eelken. He was asked, "What do you hold concerning the sacrament?"

Eelken replied, "I know nothing of your baked God." Eelken was saying that the bread itself did not turn into Jesus, but that it was a symbol of Jesus.

(from *Martyrs Mirror*, page 484)

Cheyenne Peace Chief Lawrence Hart was minister at Koinonia Mennonite Church in Oklahoma (U.S.) for over forty years. Chief Hart and his wife Betty founded the Cheyenne Cultural Center in Clinton, Oklahoma. It was important to Chief Hart to honor his Cheyenne heritage as well as embrace Anabaptist teachings. Chief Hart was present in 2005, at the first meeting of Native Mennonite Ministries, where frybread was dipped into cups for communion.

Frybread is made by frying dough in hot oil until it puffs up and turns golden brown. After the U.S. government forced Native Americans to live on land that could not grow the food they were used to, the government provided them with flour, lard, and sugar rations. Native Americans used these ingredients to make frybread.

For many Native Americans frybread is an important symbol of identity and unity. It also symbolizes their perseverance and their survival. When frybread was used for communion at the first meeting of Native Mennonite Ministries, it connected Anabaptist faith with Native American identity.

FAMILY QUESTIONS

▶ What types of bread does your family eat?

▶ Have you ever given or received a gift of bread?

▶ What different ways have you seen communion served?

Luke 22:19-20

Then he took a loaf of bread, and when he had given thanks, he broke it and gave it to them, saying, "This is my body, which is given for you. Do this in remembrance of me." And he did the same with the cup after supper, saying, "This cup that is poured out for you is the new covenant in my blood."

SHARE BREAD or crackers with each other. As you eat, consider reading one of these Bible stories together:

- 1 Kings 17:8-16 Elijah and the Widow of Zarephath
- Matthew 14:13-21 Jesus and the Feeding of the Five Thousand

MAKE IT!

Make a batch of your favorite bread, or try this recipe for fry bread.
From *Extending the Table* (page 49):

1.
Combine in large mixing bowl:
3 c flour
1 ¼ tsp baking powder
1 tsp salt
2 Tbsp dry milk powder (optional)

2.
Gradually stir in:
1 ⅓ c warm water (or slightly less)

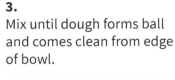

3.
Mix until dough forms ball and comes clean from edge of bowl.

4.
Knead on lightly floured surface until well mixed and elastic. Divide dough into 8 pieces and roll into balls. Using palms of hands, pat into circles about ½-inch thick.

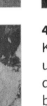

5.
Together with an adult, heat ¾ inch oil to 450 degrees in frypan. Carefully slip rounded, flat piece of dough into hot oil. Bread will start to rise to top of hot oil. When underside of bread is brown, turn over and brown other side. Drain well on paper, then place in baking pan in 200 degree oven and cover with damp towel to keep warm and chewy. Repeat with remaining dough.

—Betty E. Hart (Clinton, OK)
—Velma Heisey (Mount Joy, PA) and Nancy Heisey (Ephrata, PA)
—Myrtis Morris (Philadelphia, PA) and
   Elaine Maust (Meridian, MS)

THINK ABOUT IT!

With whom could you share this bread?

PRAYER

Thank you, God, for bread to eat and share with family and friends.

Amen

10. BELIEVERS BAPTISM

The believers church is a community of people who have chosen to live out the gospel of Jesus Christ together. For Anabaptists, believers baptism is the practice by which a youth or adult joins a believers church community. The believers church is separate from the civil government.

Baptism can happen in several ways. It may include the sprinkling or pouring of water on an individual's head; sometimes the person is immersed completely in water.

EARLY STORY

Anna Mantz lived in the city of Zurich, Switzerland, down the street from the large Grossmünster Church. On the evening of January 21, 1525, a small group of individuals gathered in Anna's house. This small group decided to take the step of adult baptism, in order to show that they were forming a believers church community that was separate from the established state church.

One of the men, George Blaurock, requested that Conrad Grebel baptize him. Then Blaurock baptized the rest of those who were present. Anna and her adult son Felix Mantz were among those who were baptized that evening.

Those who were baptized as adults eventually became known as Anabaptists, which means "baptized again."

Wenceslao Flores home, Cachipay, Colombia.

GLOBAL STORY

Wenceslao Flores and his wife, Anatilde, were some of the first Mennonite believers in Cachipay, Colombia. They regularly hosted worship services in their home for friends and neighbors. The Flores' neighbor, Anselmo, did not understand Wenceslao and Anatilde's faith, and it confused him that they had services in their home instead of a church. One day Anselmo angrily threatened Wenceslao, and the Flores family was afraid.

Soon after, however, Anselmo's wife became very ill. Wenceslao requested that the car of the Mennonite mission be used to transport his ill neighbor. The missionaries drove her to the hospital, where she soon recovered. After this, Anselmo was no longer angry, and Wenceslao began to lead their two families together in worship and Bible study. On January 1, 1953, Anselmo and Anatilde were baptized in the Cachipay River together with Anselmo and his wife.

Baptism in the river.

FAMILY QUESTIONS

▶ Have you ever seen a baptism?

▶ How is baptism practiced at your church?

▶ Has anyone in your family been baptized?

▶ Why do you think water is used in baptisms?

43

Luke 3:21-22

Now when all the people were baptized, and when Jesus also had been baptized and was praying, the heaven was opened, and the Holy Spirit descended upon him in bodily form like a dove.

APPRECIATE THE GOODNESS OF WATER TOGETHER

Option 1:
Pour a drink of water for each person in your circle. Maybe you have a favorite glass, mug, or cup to use. Perhaps you have lemon slices, mint leaves, or ice cubes to add. As you sip, think about all the places water is found in our world. What can we do to help protect water resources on the earth?

**Thank you, God,
for the rain which
waters our earth.**

Amen

TALK ABOUT IT!

Option 2:
Create a family litany, thanking God for water. Write
down a list of all the ways water is used by your family in
your home. When the list is finished, assign one person
to read down through the list, pausing after each item
so that the others can say together: "Thank you, God,
for water."

11. SERVICE TO ONE ANOTHER

To serve means to give your time, talents, and energy to help another person or help in a situation. This happens in ways both small and large. Some adults and families choose to participate in voluntary service assignments for specific periods of time. Anabaptists look to the life of Jesus in the New Testament as an example of a person who served others—even those who were excluded or appeared to be enemies.

EARLY STORY

Dirk Willems was an Anabaptist living in the city of Asperen, Netherlands. Like many other Anabaptists in the sixteenth century, his life was in danger due to his faith practices. Dirk was imprisoned but managed to flee his captors. Dirk escaped his pursuers by successfully crossing a frozen river. However, the man following him broke through a thin patch of ice and was on the verge of drowning. Dirk returned to the spot and pulled his pursuer out of the water. Though the man he saved may have been willing to let Dirk go as thanks for Dirk's help, the magistrate following them both forced the man to arrest Dirk.

(from *Martyrs Mirror*, page 741)

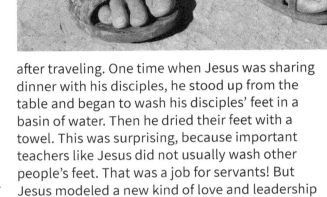

GLOBAL STORY

Mary Weaver spent over a decade as a nurse at a retirement community in Bluffton, Ohio (U.S.). One of her favorite tasks was providing foot care for the residents. Many of the elderly people there could no longer take care of their own feet. So Mary helped them. She gently bathed and dried their feet. Then she carefully trimmed their nails. Finally, she lotioned their feet, so the skin would not crack or itch.

In the time of Jesus, people walked on dry, dusty roads, and they needed their feet washed after traveling. One time when Jesus was sharing dinner with his disciples, he stood up from the table and began to wash his disciples' feet in a basin of water. Then he dried their feet with a towel. This was surprising, because important teachers like Jesus did not usually wash other people's feet. That was a job for servants! But Jesus modeled a new kind of love and leadership by washing his disciples' feet.

Mary knew that Jesus had washed his friends' feet, and she was glad that she could share Jesus' love with her residents by caring for their feet.

FAMILY QUESTIONS

▶ What are ways that your family members help each other?

▶ What are ways in which church members help each other?

▶ What are ways in which you serve in your community?

SCRIPTURE

1 Peter 4:9-10

Be hospitable to one another without complaining. Like good stewards of the manifold grace of God, serve one another with whatever gift each of you has received.

FOOTWASHING, OR POURING OF WATER OVER HANDS

To begin, read the description of footwashing found in John 13:3-5. In this passage, Jesus washes the feet of his disciples. If you choose to pour water over each other's hands, you could first talk about the ways we use our hands to serve others.

Option 1:
Wash each other's feet.
Supplies needed: large basin with two or three inches of warm water, two towels, soap (optional)

Place the water basin on one towel to keep the floor from getting slippery. As one person places her or his foot in the basin, another person can cup his or her hands to pour water over the foot or use soap to wash the foot. The second towel is to dry the foot.

Footwashing service at Kulp Theological Seminary in Kwarhi, Nigeria.

Option 2:
Pour water over each other's hands.
Supplies needed: pitcher of water, large empty basin to catch the water, two towels

Place the water basin on one towel. As one person cups her or his hands over the empty bowl, another person pours water over the hands. The second towel is to dry hands.

PRAYER

Thank you, God, for those who help and serve others.

Amen

12. STEWARDSHIP

Stewardship is the idea that our lives, our work, and our possessions are dedicated to taking care of God's kingdom. This understanding is reflected in how we use our resources. Creation stewardship may mean taking care of the earth, water, or air. Financial stewardship includes thinking about how you spend money.

EARLY STORY

Maeyken van Deventer was a sixteenth-century Anabaptist woman. While imprisoned because of her faith, she wrote a letter to her children. She encouraged them to seek the richness of life that Christian faith brings and to leave aside the pursuit of earthly wealth. Her letter included these words of explanation about sharing resources with others:

Hear, my children, the instruction of your mother, and incline your hearts to understanding, and open your ears to hear the words of my mouth...

...my children, love your neighbor heartily, and this with a liberal heart. Let the light of the Gospel shine in you. Deal your bread to the hungry, clothe the naked, and do not suffer anything to remain with you double, since there are enough that lack. And whatsoever the Lord grants you, that possess with thankfulness, not only for yourselves, but also for your neighbor, and seek not your own profit, but that of your neighbor. In short, my children, let your life be conformed to the Gospel of Christ.

(from *Martyrs Mirror*, pages 977-979)

In 2015, Américo Aji, leader of the Mennonite Brethren churches in Panama, shared this story at Mennonite World Conference Assembly gathered in Pennsylvania: "We have spent much time in prayer. Prayer for the struggle that we have experienced for many years; the struggle to have our land, and our family security. Because it is the earth, the land, that sustains us. Not only do we live from this land, but as human beings created by God, our people want to conserve everything that is created, our nature, and our environment."

The Wounaan hope to protect their land and their people. Leaders have carefully identified cocobolo trees throughout their territory and made a plan for harvesting and replanting, so that both the Wounaan communities and the trees will survive. The Panamanian Mennonite Brethren churches ask the global Anabaptist community to join them in praying for their people and their land, that all will be able to live fully and peacefully.

In Panama, as of 2018 there are thirteen Mennonite Brethren churches, mostly made up of Wounaan and Emberá peoples. The Wounaan are an indigenous group known for making carvings out of red cocobolo wood. Although the government has promised them a large tract of forested land that has historically been the home of the Wounaan, logging companies have been moving into the territory, cutting down trees, and turning the forest into fields for cattle.

As their land is taken, the Mennonite Brethren in Panama have found themselves threatened, afraid, and worried about the future of their churches and of the land.

FAMILY QUESTIONS

▶ What needs does your family have?

▶ What treasures are more important than money?

▶ In what ways does your family practice stewardship?

SCRIPTURE

Matthew 6:19-21

Do not store up for yourselves treasures on earth, where moth and rust consume and where thieves break in and steal; but store up for yourselves treasures in heaven, where neither moth nor rust consumes and where thieves do not break in and steal. For where your treasure is, there your heart will be also.

CHOOSE A STEWARDSHIP PROJECT

Option 1:
Find a jar (or basket, box, etc.) in which to collect coins. You may want to decorate the container with illustrations or a favorite scripture verse. Decide as a family where the collected coins will go: Your church offering? A local community organization? A global relief agency?

MAKE IT!

FIND IT!

Option 2:
Consider the words of Psalm 24: The earth is the Lord's and all that is in it. Take a walk in your neighborhood. What do you notice? What seasons do you experience in your part of the world? What plants and animals live near you? What kind of land and water is around you? Draw pictures of what you see.

Option 3:
Is there a patch of ground near you that needs tending? If you have space for a flower or vegetable garden, is there a way to share your harvest with others?

AFTERWORD

In a famous letter to Thomas Müntzer, written in fall 1524, Conrad Grebel, the early Swiss Anabaptist leader, cited Matthew 19:14 ("let the children come to me") in a long series of biblical passages attesting to the innocence of children. "We hold," he concluded, "that all children who have not yet attained the knowledge to distinguish between good and evil . . . are certainly saved through the suffering of Christ, the new Adam."

That conviction—that God's free gift of grace extends to children—was at the basis of the Anabaptist understanding of "believers baptism." Baptism, they believed, should be a voluntary, conscious decision; a commitment made only when one was old enough to express genuine repentance for sin and a desire to follow Christ in the path of daily discipleship.

Yet such decisions are never made in a vacuum. Even as later generations of Anabaptist-Mennonites have honored the principle of believers baptism, we have also recognized the singular importance of nurturing children in the faith. Some of the best-known letters preserved in the *Martyrs Mirror* were written by parents—imprisoned for their faith, sometimes awaiting execution—to their children, admonishing them to read Scripture and listen to the teaching of their mentors in the hopes that one day they would also choose to follow in the narrow way of Jesus.

The materials gathered together in this book beautifully illustrate these central convictions of the Anabaptist tradition. Children are both innocent before God and in need of instruction. In twelve simple, clear, and creative chapters, Lisa Weaver and Elizabeth Miller have provided a resource for families, mentors, and Sunday school teachers who are committed to nurturing the next generation of children in the basic teachings of the Christian faith. Whether or not they will eventually choose to follow Jesus is a decision each one will need to make. In the meantime, "Let the children come!"

—*John D. Roth, Director*
Institute for the Study of Global Anabaptism
"Bearing Witness"

SUGGESTIONS FOR USE IN CHRISTIAN EDUCATION

These twelve units are easily adapted for use in a Sunday School classroom or at a congregational, conference, or camp retreat. As it is often helpful for children if routines are established, the following simple outline is recommended for use in a group setting.

GATHERING
As children enter the room, greet each student by name, and invite her or him to join the others at a welcoming spot (rug or table). At this space, students can do a quiet activity until everyone is present. Suggestions include: playdough, puzzles, drawing, or looking at picture books.

OPENING
Invite the children to your storytelling space. Introduce the theme (eg. prayer, communion, stewardship) and ask what the children know of that word. Accept all shared thoughts and connections. Share a simple definition, and if possible, give examples of how your congregation members engage in this practice.

STORYTELLING
Tell the children that you will be sharing two stories—one from the sixteenth century and one from current times. Also, the stories will be taking place in two different areas of the world. Ask the children to listen for ways in which the two stories are alike and different. Take time to wonder about the stories together.

If desired, use small figures or objects to help children visualize each story. Beautiful wooden figures can be purchased at a fair-trade venue such as Ten Thousand Villages, or you can simply create a cast of characters from among the little toy people found in your home. Another option is to create characters out of pipe cleaners or clay, if you are so inclined.

A scene for each story can be established using a placemat for each setting. In other words, tell the first story using one set of figures on one placemat. Leave that scene set up, and tell the second story using a different set of figures and a different placemat.

DISCUSSION

Ask children how the stories were alike and different. Ask how each story is related to the theme. Use the Family Questions as further talking points.

ACTIVITY

Choose one or more of the activity suggestions that fit the size and needs of your class. There is a wide range of activity options; some require preparation ahead of time, including the gathering of materials.

SCRIPTURE

Regather the children in your storytelling space. Express your joy in being with them during Sunday School, and read to them the scripture verse. Or, if children have their own Bibles and are of reading age, you can all locate and read the verse together.

CLOSING PRAYER:

As a final community experience, say the closing prayer together. Options would include:

▶ Join hands, and have an adult read the prayer.

▶ Have an adult say a phrase, and have children echo line by line.

▶ Write the prayer on a poster board, and have a child read the prayer, or have everyone read it together.

FURTHER SUGGESTIONS:

▶ Create a bulletin board using a map of the world. Each week, mark the location of the stories.

▶ Set out the storytelling figures and placemats at the Gathering time. Children love to tell and retell stories with characters. They may choose to retell stories from previous lessons, or stories of their own creation.

▶ Choose a favorite song to use each week. You can sing or play it when you gather for storytelling at the beginning of the lesson or as part of the closing prayer time.

NOTES

ACKNOWLEDGMENTS

The authors wish to express deep appreciation to:

- Designer Judith Rempel Smucker, for her artistic vision and collaborative spirit

- All the individuals who shared stories, photos, and artwork

- John D. Roth and the *Bearing Witness Story Project,* provider of generous financial support and content

- All reviewers of the manuscript, including Carissa Christner, J. Denny Weaver, and Malinda Berry

- Editor Michael A. King, who provided prompt support and professional oversight throughout the project

- Jonathan Dyck and Neil Richer, who supported us in carving out time for writing, compiling, editing, talking, and thinking about this project

- Our children, in various life stages, who keep our faith fresh with their questions, perspectives, and presence

- All those around the world who nurture the faith development of children

Credits and Permissions

Listed below are sources (artistic works, written texts, interviews) which were used by the authors. Permissions were secured for the use of images. Photos of artwork were taken by Jonathan Dyck and Judith Rempel Smucker unless otherwise noted. The authors will gladly receive information that will enable them to rectify inadvertent omissions or errors in future editions. Early stories were primarily drawn from the following two sources:

Martyrs Mirror by Thieleman J. van Braght. Herald Press, 1979. Etchings created by Jan Luyken.

Living the Anabaptist Story: A Guide to Early Beginnings with Questions for Today by Lisa D. Weaver and J. Denny Weaver. Cascadia Publishing House, 2015.

FRONT COVER:
Images / Rainbow artwork: Evan Rempel.

FRONT MATTER
Inside title page / Rainbow artwork: Evan Rempel.
Publication page / Hens and chicks artwork: Levi Eberly.
Table of Contents / Flower artwork: Ivan Rempel.
Introduction / Storytelling items, arranged on towel:
    Photo by Jonathan Dyck.

UNIT 1
Early story / *Martyrs Mirror,* p 482.
Global story / "An Open Bible at Rebel Headquarters," by Vincent Ndandula and Jim Bertsche in *The Jesus Tribe: Grace Stories from Congo's Mennonites, 1912-2012.* Editors Rod Hollinger-Janzen, Nancy Myers, and Jim Bertsche. Institute for Mennonite Studies, 2012: pp 82-87.
Images / Samuel Kakesa, Françoise Kafutshi, and their child: Photo provided by Africa Inter-Mennonite Mission.
Modern-day Bible, Psalm 23 scripture verse, basket with lid:
    Photos by Jonathan Dyck.
Song poster at Mosquito Hollow campfire:
    Photo by Camp Friedenswald staff of Henry Martin.
Pottery bowls: Seth Weaver.
500-year old Bible: Wikimedia Commons.

UNIT 2
Early story / *Living the Anabaptist Story*, pp 34-35.
Global story / Phone interview and email communication with Hilda Franz.
Images / Quill: Wikimedia Commons.
Hands knitting: Bigstock photos.
Two women wrapped in shawl: Photo by Mennonite Disaster Service.
Fleece blanket: Lisa Weaver.

UNIT 3
Early story / *Living the Anabaptist Story*, pp 31-32.
Global story / Adapted from "Thousands Celebrate Milestone, Christ" by Ryan Miller in Mennonite Mission Network News (online), March 2, 2008.
Images / Mela in Parrapat, India: Photo by David Fast.
Modern-day staff: Photo by Judith Rempel Smucker.
Accordion card: Lydia Siegrist.
Dolphin pop-up card: Makai Cummings.
Flower pop-up card: Lisa Weaver.

UNIT 4
Early story / *Martyrs Mirror*, pp 563-568.
Global story / "Hugo Donatti" on Global Anabaptist Wiki (anabaptistwiki.org). Additional email communication with John Driver and Hugo Donatti (via translator Milka Rindzinski).
Images / Stack of books, flags: Bigstock photos.
Flashlight, star ornament, sentence starters, candle on mat:
    Photos by Jonathan Dyck.

UNIT 5
Early story / *Martyrs Mirror,* p 477.
Global story / Email interview and additional communication with William Kulepeta (via translator Suzanne Lind).
Images / Pieter Pieters Beckjen: *Martyrs Mirror,* p 739.
Musicians (left to right) Ciril Ebala, William Kulepeta, Exoce Fumana: Photo by Suzanne Lind.
    Drummer Rev. Mumba Kabula: Photo by Nancy Myers.
Child and tree at Camp Friedenswald:
    Photo by Peter H. Ringenberg.
Child in blanket house:
    Photo by Malinda Berry of Jeremiah Stoltzfus.
Journal with pencil: Photo by Jonathan Dyck.
Campfire artwork: Avery Rempel.
Child writing in journal: Istock photo.

UNIT 6
Early story / *The Complete Writings of Menno Simons, c. 1496-1561.* Translated from the Dutch by Leonard Verduin and edited by J. C. Wenger. Herald Press, 1956: pp 198, 554.
Global story / Interview with Norris Glick, son of Melvin Ira Glick.
Images / Engraving of Menno Simons: Menno Simons, wt Friesland : [Amsterdam] CVSichem inuent. scul. et excud. [1608-1677]. Call number OTM: Pr. K 600A (University of Amsterdam, Netherlands).
Holding hands: Bigstock photo.
Art supplies, "Love your neighbor" banner, scripture verses:
    Photos by Jonathan Dyck.
Peace-sign footsteps, "The Golden Rule" artwork: Avery Rempel.
"Justicia Económica" banner: Photo by Anna Vogt.

UNIT 7

Early story / *Martyrs Mirror,* pp 546-547.
Global story / Presentation by a pastor from Ethiopia at the Bearing
   Witness consultation, August 5-12, 2012. Goshen College,
   Indiana, United States.
*Beyond Our Prayers: An Amazing Half-Century of Church Growth
   in Ethiopia, 1948-199*8 by Nathan B. Hege. Herald Press, 1998.
Images / Prison bars of Jacob de Roore: *Martyrs Mirror,* p 775.
   Children after worship at Meserete Kristos Church:
   Photo by Darrell Jantzi, as seen in *Canadian Mennonite,*
   November 14, 2017.
Meserete Kristos Church, Addis Ababa:
   Mennonite World Conference photo/*Courier* 25.3/4.
Handwritten verse (John 14:6): Levi Behrens.
Orange pocket, scripture verses: Photos by Jonathan Dyck.
Hands passing slip of paper: Bigstock photo.

UNIT 8

Early story / *Martyrs Mirror,* pp 453-454.
Global story / Bearing Witness interview with Naomi Tamura,
   July 23, 2015. Video interview with Naomi can be found at www.
   martyrstories.org/naomi-tamura-japan.
Images / Anna Jansz of Rotterdam: *Martyrs Mirror,* p 453.
Naomi Tamura gathered with her congregation in Japan:
   Photo provided by Naomi Tamura.
Drawing with stick in sand: Istock photo.
Nativity figures, towel on mat, walnut, pipe cleaner boat:
   Photos by Jonathan Dyck.
Origami boat and instructions: Judith Rempel Smucker.

UNIT 9

Early story / *Martrys Mirror,* pp 481-484.
Global story / *Searching for Sacred Ground: The Journey of Chief
   Lawrence Hart, Mennonite* by Raylene Hinz-Penner. Cascadia
   Publishing House, 2007: 139.
"Native American Fry Bread" recipe from *Extending the Table*,
   Revised Edition. Herald Press, 2014: 48.
Jen Miller, "Frybread," Smithsonian.com (July 2008),
   https://www.smithsonianmag.com/arts-culture/frybread-79191/.
Images / Wooden communion cup, Muddy Creek Farm Library
   of Ephrata, Pennsylvania: Photo by Julie Kauffman.
Top three bread photos: Wikimedia Commons.
Fry bread on plate, and steps for making fry bread:
   Photos by Elizabeth Miller of Laurel Richer.
Extending the Table recipe book cover: Herald Press, 2014.

UNIT 10

Early story / *Living the Anabaptist Story*, p 22.
Global story / "The Gospel Changes a Would-Be Murderer,"
   Colombian News 4 (1 Jan 1953), 2.

Images / Baptism scene: From Hortensius, *Het boeck van den
   oproer,* University of Amsterdam. Etching after painting by
   Barent Dirks, destroyed in 1652. Special Collections, University of
   Amsterdam, Netherlands, OTM: Pr. K 855a.
Wenceslao Flores home, baptism in river:
   Photos provided by Peter Stucky.
"Thank you, God, for water" artwork: Ben Siegrist.
Water cups and mint leaves: Photos by Jonathan Dyck.
Waterfall: Photo by Anna Vogt.
Handwritten list of water uses: Rachel Behrens.

UNIT 11

Early story / *Martyrs Mirror,* p 741.
Global story / Interview with Mary Lois Wenger Weaver.
Images / Dirk Willems: *Martyrs Mirror*, p 741.
Feet in sandals, feet in slippers: Bigstock photos.
Towel on mat: Photo by Jonathan Dyck.
Footwashing at Kulp Theological Seminary in Kwarhi, Nigeria:
   Photo by Nathan and Jennifer Hosler, Copyright Church of the
   Brethren.
Children pouring water:
   Photos by Lisa Weaver of Isadora Christner and Gabriel Christner.

UNIT 12

Early story / *Martyrs Mirror,* pp 977-979.
Global story / Bearing Witness interview with Américo Aji,
   July 23, 2015.
Video: Mennonite World Conference, "MWC Delegation to
   Panama," *YouTube*, 20 April 2015, https://www.youtube.com/
   watch?v=W7NXc6pDNjU&t=74s.
"Mennonites in Panama Oppose Clear-Cutting, Request Prayer"
   by Will Braun in *Canadian Mennonite*, Sept 9, 2015.
Images / Wounaan congregation in Panama:
   Photo by Henk Stenvers.
Jar with coins, garden: Photos by Jonathan Dyck.
Box with coins: Photo by Judith Rempel Smucker.
Accordion card: Lydia Siegrist.
Tree artwork: Levi Behren.

BACK MATTER:

Images / Drawing of two people: Avery Rempel.
Animal figures: Photo by Lisa Weaver.
"Have a good day" sign: Painting by Emma Neff-Mallon;
   Photo by Kent Sweitzer.

BACK COVER:

Images / Children looking at lantern: Photo by Malinda Berry
   of Jeremiah Stoltzfus and Chloe Stoltzfus.

Lightning Source UK Ltd.
Milton Keynes UK
UKHW050304250820
368755UK00003B/123